FORCED VACCINATIONS
THINKING BIBLICALLY

SCOTT T. BROWN

Church &
Family Life

Forced Vaccinations: Thinking Biblically
by Scott T. Brown
First Printing: September 2021

All Scripture quotations, unless otherwise indicated, are taken from the New King James Version.

Church & Family Life
220 South White St., Wake Forest, NC 27587
www.churchandfamilylife.com

ISBN: 978-1-62418-065-1
Cover Design and Typography by Justin Turley
Printed in the United States of America

OTHER BOOKS BY
CHURCH AND FAMILY LIFE

CONTENTS

INTRODUCTION

The focus of everything I say here is to proclaim Christ's authority over your body in the face of forced vaccination mandates. Christ is the Head of the church (Eph. 1:22; 5:23; Col. 1:18). He rules over every part of our lives. As God explains in His Word, He has instituted various jurisdictions or spheres of authority on earth. It is essential that we think biblically about these jurisdictions and how these God-ordained jurisdictions have been designed for the glory of God; for "the Holy Scripture is the only sufficient, certain, and infallible rule of all saving knowledge, faith and obedience."[1]

There are six headings under which I have organized my thoughts on this subject:

1. Ownership—the starting principle
2. Thinking Christianly about jurisdictions
3. The Sixth Commandment and God's command to take good care of your body
4. The Ninth Commandment and particpating in lies about Covid-19
5. Resistance
6. The truth about you and the authority of God

---

1 The 1677/89 London Baptist Confession of Faith: Thirty-Two Articles of Christian Faith and Practice with Scripture Proofs Adopted by the Ministers and Messengers of the General Assembly Which Met in London in 1689, n.d.

LAYING A HISTORICAL FOUNDATION

This is not the first time in history that vaccines have been mandated or have been threatened to be mandated. Compulsory vaccination is nothing new. Over two hundred years ago, George Washington ordered his troops to be vaccinated against smallpox in 1777. This was done because the armies were losing so many men to smallpox. Thirty years later, the first vaccine mandate in the United States was entered into law in 1809 when Boston imposed mandatory smallpox vaccinations on its inhabitants.[2]

In 1855, the state of Massachusetts mandated smallpox vaccinations as a requirement for school attendance. By 1900, thirteen other states had followed suit.[3] Still today, public schools require vaccinations.

In 1905, the Supreme Court upheld a state's right to require compulsory vaccinations to protect the health of its citizens in *Jacobson v. Massachusetts*. In this case, the Court stated: "The police power of a State embraces such reasonable regulations . . . as will protect the public health and safety."[4]

---

2   "The U.S. Has a Long Precedent for Vaccine Mandates," NPR, August 29, 2021, https://www.npr.org/2021/08/29/1032169566/the-u-s-has-a-long-precedent-for-vaccine-mandates; Cristina Valldejuli, "When Did Mandatory Vaccinations Become Common?" History News Network, Columbian College of Arts and Sciences, March 18, 2015, https://historynewsnetwork.org/article/158827.

3   René F. Najera, "Timeline of Vaccination Mandates," College of Physicians of Philadelphia, August 9, 2021, https://historyofvaccines.blog/2021/08/09/timeline-of-vaccination-mandates/.

4   *Jacobson v. Massachusetts*, https://tile.loc.gov/storage-services/service/ll/usrep/usrep197/usrep197011/usrep197011.pdf.

As can be seen, vaccination mandates are nothing new in United States history. But with each new mandate, a cultural upheaval has always ensued. Vaccination debates go back as far as the dawn of the vaccine movement in the 1720's when smallpox was killing countless numbers across the nation.[5] Pastors got involved in the debate. Such prominent brethren as Jonathan Edwards, Cotton and Increase Mather, and others became embroiled in the controversy. The debates were vigorous to say the least, and at times they were perhaps even slanderous. The consequences were significant. Johnathan Edwards and his daughter both died of the smallpox vaccine.

WHY ARE PEOPLE OBJECTING TO THESE VACCINES?

Why are people objecting to the Covid-19 vaccine? There appear to be two groups who are resisting the current vaccination mandates. One group are historical anti-vaxxers. They are opposed to vaccines—period. They believe that modern vaccines often carry serious side effects, including autism and various forms of allergies.

A NEW GROUP HAS EMERGED

But a new group has recently emerged. These are not anti-vaxxers. They aren't opposed to vaccines in general, but they are opposed to the Covid-19 vaccines currently on the market. They are fearful of these vaccines. Why?

---

5   Maggie Astor, "Vaccination Mandates Are an American Tradition. So Is the Backlash," *The New York Times*, September 9, 2021, https://www.nytimes.com/2021/09/09/us/politics/vaccine-mandates-history.html; Shawn Buhr, "To Inoculate or Not to Inoculate? The Debate and the Smallpox Epidemic of Boston in 1721," *Constructing the Past*: Vol. 1, Iss. 1, Article 8, https://digitalcommons.iwu.edu/constructing/vol1/iss1/8.

First, Covid-19 vaccines were released to the public more quickly than any other vaccination through "Operation Warp Speed." Most vaccines are tested for 8-10 years on average before being released to the public. Through Operation Warp Speed, Covid-19 vaccines bypassed these safety measures and were released prior to undergoing the standard rigorous testing required of other vaccines. Because Coronavirus vaccines received no long-term testing, they can provide no track record to ensure they are devoid of serious long-term effects.

Second, these vaccines employ new technologies. The mRNA vaccine operates differently than traditional vaccines.[6] Because it uses a new technology, people are fearful of the unknown and prefer not to put their health at risk by getting the vaccination.

Third, the CDC is reporting a significantly higher number of people who experience adverse reactions to the Covid-19 vaccine when compared to other vaccines. This number is four hundred times higher than previous vaccines.[7]

Because of these factors, Covid-19 vaccines are being resisted like no other vaccine in history. Does this resistance rest on a biblical foundation? How should we as Christians think about these vaccines? What should be our response to them? These are the questions I seek to answer in this booklet.

---

6   "Understanding mRNA COVID-19 Vaccines," Centers for Disease Control and Prevention, March 4, 2021, https://www.cdc.gov/coronavirus/2019-ncov/vaccines/different-vaccines/mrna.html.

7   Megan Redshaw, "VAERS data released today by the CDC showed a total of 441,931 reports of adverse events from all age groups following COVID vaccines, including 6,985 deaths and 34,065 serious injuries between Dec. 14, 2020 and June 25, 2021," Rights and Freedoms, July 2, 2021, https://rightsfreedoms.wordpress.com/2021/07/03/as-adverse-reactions-to-covid-vaccines-reach-400000-the-truth-must-be-spread-widely/.

—|—

OWNERSHIP:
THE STARTING PRINCIPLE

My intention within this booklet is to proclaim the governance and rule of the Lord Jesus Christ—and Him alone—over every aspect of our lives. In order to frame the discussion and point it in the direction in which it ought to be directed, I want to begin by quoting three passages of Scripture. The first is from Isaiah 43:1:

> But now, thus says the LORD, who created you, O Jacob, and He who formed you, O Israel: "Fear not, for I have redeemed you; I have called you by your name; **You are Mine.**"

"You are Mine." These are the words of the Lord God, the Creator of heaven and earth.

The second text confronts us with the necessity of examining our own hearts. Matthew 22:36-37 says:

> "Teacher, which is the great commandment in the law?" Jesus said to him, " 'You shall love the LORD your God with all your heart, with all your soul, and with all your mind.' "

Do you love the Lord with your whole heart? Do you embrace God's claim on your whole life?

This brings us to the third text, which is the first commandment of the law. Exodus 20:3 states, "You shall have no other gods before Me."

This is the starting principle. You and I were created by God. We have been made in God's image. This gives God full claim on our lives. This command does not teach that God is my first priority, my family is my second priority, and my work is my third priority. No, this proclaims that there is only one priority, and it is to love God with everything we are. As Paul says, "To live is Christ" (Phil. 1:21). That, in a nutshell, is what I want to proclaim in this booklet on jurisdictions and forced vaccinations.

My focus of this booklet is to define the jurisdictional responsibility we have over our own healthcare and to declare God's governance and rule over every part of our lives.

THINKING BIBLICALLY
ABOUT JURISDICTIONS

How does one think biblically (or "Christianly") about forced vaccinations or any mandate that encroaches on your personal rights of decision on what you put in or on your body?

We live in a moment when we're experiencing governmental and institutional tyranny like we've never seen before. Civil governments are threatening us, telling us to do things we never imagined anyone would ever tell us to do. Last year, our government told us to shut down our churches, stay away from one another and wear masks. Now they are telling us that we must be vaccinated multiple times using a new technology. What should we as Christians think about this? How should we respond?

NOT A MEDICAL ANALYSIS

Let me be clear. I am not analyzing vaccines in this booklet. While I have grave medical concerns regarding the current injections that are being forced upon us, I'm not here as a doctor to tell you what you need to know about vaccines. I'm not arguing about whether you should take the vaccine. Do your own research about the vaccine and come to your own conclusions. Whatever you do, do it by faith, for whatever is not from faith is sin (Rom. 14:23).

What I would like to do is to help you think through the biblical principles regarding mandates and governmental intrusion on the matter of forced vaccinations. It is important that we do this now because we are seeing medical and governmental tyranny in America like never before.

What follows are some principles to help you think through these mandates from a biblical perspective. It is very important that we learn how to think like Christians.

The fundamental principle is this: God alone has all authority in heaven and on earth. He has created all earthly authorities and jurisdictions in this world. The authority of earthly rulers is real, but it is only real because this authority has been delegated to them by God. God requires these earthly authorities to rule according to His Word and within the limited bounds He has established for them. God has set both positive duties and clearly defined limitations to each of these authorities. This delegated authority has been instituted by God as a means of establishing His order on earth (Ps. 2:10-12; Isa. 9:6-7; Isa. 33:22; Matt. 28:18; Rom. 13:1-2; Eph. 6:5-8; Col. 1:15-20; 1 Pet. 2:13-14, 18).

God has created five separate jurisdictions: the family, the church, the civil government, the individual and the employer. Each has its own responsibilities and sphere of authority. Thinking of the world this way is to think biblically and Christianly.

THINKING BIBLICALLY

How do we learn to think like Christians? Simply put, whenever we consider any issue, we scan the pages of Scripture for wisdom. We look not to our background, culture, government, philosophers or our previous thoughts. We look to Scripture alone; we look to God who created us and who has given us the revelation of Himself through His holy Word. We have been given all we need for life and godliness—not in ourselves, but in the Word of God: "All Scripture is given by inspiration of God, and is profitable for doctrine, for reproof, for correction, for instruction in righteousness, that the man of God may be complete, thoroughly equipped for every good work" (2 Tim. 3:16-17). We embrace the truth that "Man shall not live by bread alone, but by every word that proceeds from the mouth of God" (Deut. 8:3; Matt. 4:4). It is truth from the Spirit of God that we need. "It is the Spirit who gives life; the flesh profits nothing. The words that I speak to you are spirit, and they are life" (John 6:63; see also John 15:1-5; Eph. 1:3; Heb. 4:12; Jas. 1:17).

Thinking biblically includes renouncing the worldly philosophies that are constantly driving our culture: "Beware lest anyone cheat you through philosophy and empty deceit, according to the tradition of men, according to the basic principles of the world, and not according to Christ. For in Him dwells all the fullness of the Godhead bodily; and you are complete in Him, who is the head of all principality and power" (Col. 2:8). We must have nothing to do with personal autonomy, with man setting his own mind and understanding above the wisdom of the Word of God. We are not independent. We must renounce the popular position of "my truth" and instead embrace God's truth.

FIVE JURISDICTIONS

Let's look briefly at the responsibilities God has given each of the five jurisdictions.

First, the family is charged to establish the lordship of Christ in the home, be fruitful and multiply, raise children in the training and admonition of the Lord, and prepare generations to see the beauty of the Lord (Num. 30; Deut. 6:1-9; Ps. 78:1-8; Eph. 5:22-33; 6:1-4; 1 Pet. 3:1-12).

Second, the church is charged to spread the Gospel, nourish the saints and discipline its members who are walking contrary to godliness (Matt. 18:15-20; 28:18-20; Acts 2:38; 1 Cor. 5:7-12; 2 Cor. 2:5-8; Eph. 1:22; 2:20-22; Heb. 10:24-25; 4:1-16; 13:17; 1 Pet. 2:9-10)

Third, the civil government is charged to appoint righteous rulers, bear the sword, punish evildoers and do good (Ex. 18:21; Deut. 1:13; Deut. 17:18-20; Ps. 2:10-12; Rom. 13:1, 4; Tit. 3:1; 1 Pet. 2:13-17).

Fourth, the individual is charged to maintain one's own mind and body under the authority of God (Rom. 6:19; 12:1; 1 Cor. 6:15, 18-20; 1 Thess. 4:4; 1 Pet. 2:11-12).

Fifth, the employer is charged to transact business, employing people according to the ethical commands of God (Eph. 6:5-9; 1 Pet. 2:18-25).

The biblical premise is that God has established various jurisdictions. No jurisdiction has the authority to usurp the role or responsibilities of any other jurisdiction (2 Chron. 26:16-18). If we understand this premise, we can see that forced vaccination is not a small issue.

The present crisis over forced vaccinations has occurred because one jurisdiction has stepped out of its divinely defined role into another role. In the case of civil government-mandated vaccines, one jurisdiction (the government) is forcing a needle and an experimental technology on two other jurisdictions (the individual and the family) through means of government employees, the military and executive orders.

In the case of employer-mandated vaccines, one jurisdiction is forcing a needle on two other jurisdictions (the individual and the family) through induction and retention policies.

This is an issue of great importance because it calls into question the order established by God for His created world.

Civil magistrates forcing a vaccine on individuals and families overthrows the legitimacy of the jurisdictional boundaries instituted by our Creator.

As Christians, we are subjects of the King of kings, who requires us to uphold biblical jurisdictional authority. We are required to uphold the order God placed in the world. The glory of God requires it.

When faced with a mandate requiring forced vaccinations, we must address the root of the issue. This root is jurisdictional.

God is the supreme authority. Has God given the civil government or the employer the right to require vaccinations and to mandate diet and healthcare? No! If the government or the employer tells you to drink Coke once a day or to get a vaccine, are you required to do so? Is this what Romans 13 and other passages of Scripture teach regarding the authority of the civil government and employers?

These questions strike at the heart of God's authority. They unravel the order God has established in the world. They dismiss God Himself—the God who is the Author of freedom under His holy and superior laws. They destroy both the liberty and the authority of individuals and family.

These questions strike at the heart of the jurisdictional order God has set in place in the world.

Someone might object that Matthew 22:18-21 commands us to do whatever the government tells us to do, including getting a vaccine. "Render unto Caesar the things that are Caesar's, and to God the things that are God's" (Matt. 22:21). The only problem with this argument is that our bodies don't belong to Caesar. They belong to God. (Our children don't belong to Caesar either; they also belong to God.) A Christian should not willingly give up his body to the control of Caesar. For this reason, we must wholeheartedly resist forced medical treatments.

WHOSE DECISION IS IT?

If God didn't give civil governments and employers the right to demand vaccinations, diet and healthcare of their citizens and employees, to whom did He give this right? The answer is surprisingly simple: He gave this authority to the individual, under God. God has given the individual the right, and solemn duty, to decide for himself what he will choose for his diet and healthcare and whether or not he will be vaccinated.

God by His own authority has given man jurisdictional freedom over his own health, and He has given fathers and mothers lovingly administered authority over their families. These are delegated authorities.

It is very simple. Neither your body nor the bodies of your children belong to Caesar. Neither your body nor the bodies of your children belong to an employer.

Further, your body doesn't even belong to you. It belongs to God (1 Cor. 6:20). And God has given you the authority and responsibility to treat your body well. We must treat our bodies the way God has commanded us to treat them. We have personal responsibility over the health of our bodies.

SIX BIBLICAL TEXTS TO SHAPE YOUR THINKING ABOUT YOUR OWN BODIES AND THE BODIES OF YOUR WIVES AND CHILDREN

First, governing your body is clearly commanded:

Or do you not know that your body is the temple of the Holy Spirit who is in you, whom you have from God, and you are not your own? For you were bought at a price; therefore glorify God in your body and in your spirit, which are God's (1 Corinthians 6:19-20).

Your body isn't your own. As Christians, we aren't free to do with our bodies whatever we please. We must keep our bodies in a particular way (1 Thess. 4:4).

But don't forget this includes how you cultivate your mind and every part of your life. Treat your mind, your body and your soul well. Feed it the finest of wheat (Ps. 81:16).

We may be deeply conflicted about a forced vaccine. Are we considering God's claims on our bodies when we make a decision regarding forced vaccinations? Is our decision consistent with how we view God's claims on the rest of our lives? If you are opposed to the harm of a vaccine, are you also opposed to the harm of the ungodly entertainments you might engage in? Are you opposed to the silly humor you're tempted to saturate your mind with? Are you as concerned about your mind as you are about your body?

Second, the Christian has a duty before God to render his body as a living sacrifice to God:

I beseech you therefore, brethren, by the mercies of God, that you present your bodies a living sacrifice, holy, acceptable to God, which is your reasonable service (Romans 12:1-2).

What you do with your body is an act of worship. If what you're doing with your body can't be categorized as loving God, you shouldn't be doing it.

No matter what we do with our bodies, we must do it as an act of worship, love and obedience to God. Pleasing God must be considered even in the choices we make about what we ingest into our bodies. God gave us bodies to be offered as living sacrifices to Him who made us.

Third, what you ingest into your body is not neutral:

Therefore, whether you eat or drink, or whatever you do, do all to the glory of God (1 Corinthians 10:31).

Glorifying God must be considered even in the way we view what we ingest into our bodies. Whatever we eat or drink, the Lord wants us to ask whether it glorifies Him. All of this is to be done by faith, "But he who doubts is condemned if he eats, because he does not eat from faith; for whatever is not from faith is sin" (Rom. 14:23). It pleases God when we live by faith in His everlasting Name, "But without faith it is impossible to please Him, for he who comes to God must believe that He is, and that He is a rewarder of those who diligently seek Him" (Heb. 11:6). How we treat our body and what we ingest is never neutral.

Fourth, the health and wellbeing of our bodies is important to God:

Beloved, I pray that you may prosper in all things and be in health, just as your soul prospers (3 John 1:2).

In this verse the apostle John prays for the physical health of his readers. He was mindful of their physical condition. He wanted them to prosper in physical health. He was not simply concerned about the state of their souls. He was also concerned about the state and health of their bodies. We may have the idea that God is only concerned about our souls. This is thinking like Gnostics, not Christians. The health and wellbeing of our bodies is important to God.

Fifth, Daniel did not believe the civil government had the right to demand a particular diet of its citizens:

> *But Daniel purposed in his heart that he would not defile himself with the portion of the king's delicacies, nor with the wine which he drank; therefore he requested of the chief of the eunuchs that he might not defile himself (Daniel 1:8).*

The example of Daniel in Babylon relates directly to ingesting substances into the body.

This situation is an example of tyranny over the body. King Nebuchadnezzar demanded a certain diet. Nebuchadnezzar commanded Daniel and his friends to eat the king's food. They refused.

Daniel recognized that God had given him personal jurisdiction over his own body. He was not his own (1 Cor. 6:19-20). He refused to submit to the king's unjust command, and he appealed to the authorities (Dan. 1:8).

Throughout history we find examples of governmental tyranny over the bodies of private citizens. One example of this tyranny comes to us from communist China. For dozens of years, families in China were limited to a single child. This tyrannical law was a clear violation of the biblical mandate of Genesis: "Be fruitful and multiply" (Gen. 2:27). China recently raised the number to three children. This is still tyranny. God has not given the civil government any jurisdiction over the size of one's family.

The history of Daniel in Babylon makes it clear that a government which dictates your diet is tyrannical and should be resisted.

Sixth, God has given man responsibility to take care of his own body:

> . . . that each of you should know how to possess his own vessel in sanctification and honor (1 Thessalonians 4:4).

Your body is an instrument of God. In this verse, Paul uses the term vessel. The Greek word for vessel refers to material that is useful for service, a "utensil," a "container." Using our bodies as an instrument in the Lord's service is a personal duty that God requires.

When a government or an employer demands that every person eat a particular food or be injected with an experimental vaccine, that government is usurping personal jurisdictional freedom over the care of your body.

God has granted powers to each of the five jurisdictions. He has not granted the government or the employer authority over what we eat and drink and inject into our bodies. Civil government is limited in its sphere of authority. Romans 13 describes the things civil government is limited to. Forcing a vaccine into our bodies is not one of those things. God has given man responsibility to take care of his own body.

WHY?

Why didn't God give civil government the authority to force us to inject something into our bodies? Perhaps one reason is that each person's body is different and reacts differently to various intrusions into its system. When it comes to the health and physical makeup of our bodies, we aren't all created equal.

COLLECTIVIST OR INDIVIDUALIZED HEALTHCARE

There's much talk today about collectivist healthcare. What is collectivism? Collectivism is the principle that the group takes priority over the individual.

The collectivist demands the same treatment for all, irrespective of environmental differences, genetic variations and cultural distinctions. The idea of equal healthcare for all might appear sensible at first sight, but this mindset is diametrically opposed to all accepted medical practice.[1] The medical community has always acknowledged that every person requires individualized treatment.

Let me illustrate. When you go to a doctor for treatment and that doctor wants to prescribe a particular medication, what question does that doctor ask? He asks you if you are allergic to a particular medicine before he prescribes it.

People have different constitutions. Their bodies react differently to various elements. They are allergic to different things. I once had an intern who had a peanut allergy. His body would react violently when exposed to peanuts. Some people's bodies go into shock when they eat peanuts. It would have been unloving for me to force my intern to eat peanuts.

There is no one-size-fits-all approach when it comes to healthcare or dietary needs.

We must also recognize that there is a massive philosophical system behind the idea of collectivist healthcare. If you were to use a synonym finder on your computer, what results would

---

1   See, for example, American Chemical Society, "Uncovering a New Reason Why Patients Respond Differently to the Same Drug Dose," Science News, January 16, 2007, https://www.sciencedaily.com/releases/2007/01/070115094244.htm; "Treatment and Survivorship," USCF Helen Diller Family Comprehensive Cancer Center, https://cancer.ucsf.edu/breastcarecenter/treatment.

come up when you type in collectivism? Common synonyms are, "Leninism, Marxism, Bolshevism, Maoism, collective ownership, state ownership." The collectivist mentality is the culture of the totalitarian state, not of Christian culture.

In healthcare, individualized diagnosis and guided therapy is standard medical procedure. The collectivization of healthcare—in which every person is required to have the same treatment—contradicts common sense and accepted medical wisdom. Such healthcare is unsound and should be rejected. Thus, the practice of individualized healthcare is necessary and must be preserved.

LOVING OUR NEIGHBOR

Consider the elementary principle of loving our neighbor. We each react to various foods, drinks, and injections in different ways. Some people love coffee; others get a headache whenever they drink it. This illustration could be multiplied across multitudes of foods and medicines. If coffee gives you a headache, it would be unloving for me to require you to drink it. If you have an allergic reaction to penicillin, it's not loving for me to force you to take it.

This is why God gave you personal jurisdiction over your own body. Medical treatments must be customized.

This is why good doctors consider allergies, personal health history, genetics, lifestyle diseases and conditions, the differences between males and females and your body's compatibility with medications you are already taking, etc.

One-size-fits-all medical treatment is something the medical community does not embrace, and neither should we.

COERCION AND EXTORTION

As the above Scriptures demonstrate, God has given you personal responsibility over your own body. It is therefore a usurpation of power for any other person, institution or government agency to attempt to assume that responsibility for you. Yet this is exactly what is being attempted with forced vaccinations. We are now being coerced, intimidated, pressured, shamed, threatened and compelled to inject a biological agent of unknown present and future impact into our bodies.

Please don't misunderstand me. You are free to consider the pros and cons of this vaccine and make an informed decision about whether you choose to be vaccinated. But the civil government does not possess the jurisdiction to make that decision for you. This is tyranny, and I expect that this is only the beginning of greater tyrannies.

CONSIDERATION OF PERSONAL CIRCUMSTANCES

Everyone has customized considerations. My situation will be different than yours. You may make a different decision based on your body, your skills, your family, your financial needs or other matters too numerous to mention.

I'm not arguing that it is sinful to get the vaccine. I'm saying that this decision is yours alone. You should educate yourself in what the risks are before you do so. Carefully consider the matter before you proceed. And, whether you decide to get the vaccination or not, make that decision based on your conviction that by doing so you are honoring God and acknowledging His possession of your body.

WHO OWNS YOUR BODY?

When a civil government or a commercial company forces treatments on us, they are claiming ownership of our bodies. This makes us creatures of the state or the corporation. This puts us in subjection to powerful companies. This makes us robots of the commercial medical industrial complex. This is wrong, and it should be resisted.

This is not a new problem created by the Covid-19 crisis. There is nothing new under the sun. Abraham Kuyper, writing in 1880, speaks of why vaccine mandates and certificates should be rejected out of hand.

> *For this reason, compulsory cowpox vaccination should be out of the question. Our physicians may be mistaken, and government may never stamp a particular medical opinion as orthodox and therefore binding. Moreover, compulsion can never be justified until the illness manifests itself and may therefore never be prescribed as a preventative. A third reason is that government should keep its hands off our bodies. Fourthly, government must respect conscientious objections.*
>
> *Vaccination certificates will therefore have to go— and will be gone at least from our free schools. The form of tyranny hidden in these vaccination certificates is just as real a threat to the nation's spiritual resources as a smallpox epidemic itself.[2]*

Christians need to maintain the biblical division of the jurisdictions established by God.

It's time to say no to forced vaccinations. I will address this in more detail later in this booklet.

---

2   Abraham Kuyper, *Our Program: A Christian Political Manifesto* (Lexham Press, 2015), 248.

— 3 —

THE SIXTH COMMANDMENT AND GOD'S COMMAND TO TAKE GOOD CARE OF YOUR BODY

Or do you not know that your body is the temple of the Holy Spirit who is in you, whom you have from God, and you are not your own? For you were bought at a price; therefore glorify God in your body and in your spirit, which are God's (1 Corinthians 6:19-20).

As we consider forced medical treatments, we must remember what it means to obey the direct commands of God. Specifically, we should consider the Sixth Commandment when discussing the topic of forced vaccinations and the prospect of introducing substances, especially experimental substances, into our bodies. This commandment calls us to take full and personal responsibility for the health of our bodies.

This command helps us think biblically about what is happening around us. It defines what love looks like. The world offers us countless definitions of love, but God's commands teach us what true love is. How can we know if we are loving someone and loving God? We keep His commands. Every law of God is a law of love (Rom. 13:8; Gal. 5:14; Jas. 2:8). If you want to love your neighbor, keep the commandments. Let's consider the Sixth Commandment.

The Sixth Commandment states, "You shall not murder" (Ex. 20:13). The Sixth Commandment is broad, encompassing more than actual murder. It regulates not only our murderous deeds but also our unkind actions, our harsh words, and our hateful thoughts (Matt. 5:21-22; Ps. 119:96). God's commandments aren't wooden. They are spiritual, and they penetrate to the deepest areas of our lives. We should always remember that there are many applications to each of the Ten Commandments.

The authors of the Westminster Larger Catechism believed that wherever God gave a positive command, there was a corresponding negative command implied, and vice versa. In other words, if we are commanded, "do not lie," we are correspondingly required to "tell the truth." We see this in the way the catechism questions are stated. They ask "what is required" of a command and then, turning the tables and addressing the implication of each commandment, they ask "what is prohibited" by the same command.

The Larger Westminster Catechism asks:

Q 68: What is required in the sixth commandment?
A: The sixth commandment requireth all lawful endeavors to preserve our own life, and the life of others.

The authors expand on the duties of the commandment, stating: "The duties required in the Sixth Commandment are, all careful studies, and lawful endeavors, to preserve the life of ourselves and others." They further note that we must abstain from all "practices, which tend to the unjust taking away the life of any," and we must maintain "a sober use of meat, drink, physical, sleep" and must consider our neighbor, "comforting and succoring the distressed, and protecting and defending the innocent."

The catechism leads us to meditate more deeply on this command, refusing to remain at a mere surface level as we consider the depth and breadth of God's command regarding life and death. In the section above, the Westminster authors are stating that believers should engage in "all careful studies and lawful endeavors to preserve the life of ourselves and others." In other words, we are required to study what we are doing to our bodies and the effects this has on our health.

When it comes to forced vaccinations, we ought to know what we are putting into our bodies—after "all careful studies." When it comes to matters of personal health, Christians ought to be aware of the substances they ingest and the impact of these substances on their own bodies.

Similarly, Dr. Albert Martin, in his book The Man of God, declares that we have a duty to maintain "the disciplines essential to the maintenance of good emotional and physical health."[1] He notes that Paul declared, "I discipline my body and keep it under control" (1 Cor. 9:27). Martin states that the redeemed body is a temple of the Holy Spirit. Based on this premise, he concludes that to allow your body to "accumulate excessive weight" compromises your duty of glorifying God in your body as stated in 1 Corinthians 6:20: "you were bought with a price, therefore glorify God in your body." Martin says,

---

1   Albert Martin, *The Man of God: His Calling and Godly Life* (Trinity Pulpit Press, 2018), Vol. 1, 403.

"I am a blood bought property."[2] He maintains that we should not be ignorant of the impact of various foods on our bodies.

Because we were created by God, our life is sacred. Our bodies are a divine gift, to be used as instruments under the government of God. Our lives and other people's lives are precious to God, so He delivers the Sixth Commandment to mankind to preserve life. How do we apply this commandment to vaccinations? Thinking Christianly about our bodies will lead us to protect and care for our bodies.

Is taking good care of your body an act of love? Is refusing to do harm to your body an act of love? Yes.

Before accepting an injection, we must consider a vaccine's potential to harm. Will this vaccine preserve life? Will this vaccine cause residual harm? Thinking biblically and Christianly means that it is legitimate to question the matter of forced injections of biological substances (with some proven negative side effects) into our bodies.

It's legitimate to question this because we have authority over our bodies. We have God's command to refrain from doing harm to our bodies and the bodies of others.

Have we weighed the health implications?

Are we risking our own immune systems?

Has the substance been tested long enough and carefully enough to identify its long-term side effects?

These questions must be asked and answered as a part of obeying the Sixth Commandment.

Should a Christian knowingly do something, eat something, or inject something into himself that might harm his body? No! This command requires us to study how we can bring benefit to our bodies and the bodies of others and to act accordingly.

2　Ibid., 318.

The Sixth Commandment requires us to take good care of our bodies. This is a sacred responsibility. We are not free to ingest things into our bodies that might harm them. And we must be very clear on this: we are free to resist those who would force us to ingest things that we believe might be harmful.

As we consider taking a vaccine or doing anything with our bodies, we must remember that God gave us bodies through which to glorify Him. He gave us bodies so that we would glorify Him. This is why Paul told the church in Corinth to pay careful attention to what they did with their bodies:

> *Therefore we make it our aim, whether present or absent, to be well pleasing to Him. For we must all appear before the judgment seat of Christ, that each one may receive the things done in the body, according to what he has done, whether good or bad (2 Cor. 5:9-10).*

As 1 Corinthians 6:20 tells us, "You are not your own, you were bought with a price."

—4—

THE NINTH COMMANDMENT AND PARTICIPATING IN LIES ABOUT COVID-19

Many people are asking, "Is our government misrepresenting the situation surrounding Covid-19 and the vaccines? Are the reported death rates reliable? Are the testing procedures reliable?" Are vaccine injuries accurately represented? Why is there so much censorship? I understand that we all have different perspectives of what is happening around us. What I am going to say here will be comfortable for those who believe that their government is lying to them on different levels about Covid-19. Others may be skeptical.

If you believe that civil governments and employers are embracing lies, the Ninth Commandment is telling you that you have particular responsibilities before God in relation to these lies.

The Ninth Commandment declares, "You shall not bear false witness against your neighbor" (Ex. 20:16).

Proverbs 12:22: "Lying lips are an abomination to the Lord, but those who deal truthfully are His delight."

Ephesians 4:25: "Therefore, putting away lying, 'Let each one of you speak truth with his neighbor,' for we are members of one another."

1 Peter 3:10: "He who would love life and see good days, let him refrain his tongue from evil, and his lips from speaking deceit."

What does it mean to bear false witness? Questions 144-145 of the Westminster Larger Catechism explain:

Q 144: What are the duties required in the ninth commandment?
A: The duties required in the ninth commandment are, the preserving and promoting of truth between man and man, . . . appearing and standing for the truth . . . in matters of judgment and justice, and in all other things whatsoever; a charitable esteem of our neighbors; . . .

Q 145: What are the sins forbidden in the ninth commandment?
A: The sins forbidden in the ninth commandment are, all prejudicing the truth, . . . giving false evidence, suborning [hiring or employing] false witnesses, wittingly appearing and pleading for an evil cause, outfacing and overbearing the truth; passing unjust sentence, calling evil good, and good evil; . . . concealing the truth, undue silence in a just cause, and holding our peace when iniquity calls for either a reproof from ourselves, or complaint to others; . . . hiding, excusing, or extenuating of sins, . . .

The catechism is making the claim that there are many ways to bear false witness. The authors are pointing out that it is possible to participate in lies without telling a bold-faced lie. We may endorse a lie by our behavior.

The question this command leads us to ask in our situation is, "Are the authorities telling the truth about tests, deaths, masks, vaccines and various other matters?" And, "Am I participating in lies?"—if indeed they are lies.

Have you been watching the news? I admit, it has been hard to know whom to believe. The constant flow of updates from the medical professionals are inconsistent with themselves. How do these reports compare with reports issued a year ago or even a month ago? Do the statements from government agencies support each other? Do they remain consistent? Do they make sense? Are they true? Perhaps the most flattering thing you can say about the information issuing from the government since the start of the pandemic is that it has been contradictory.

WHOM DO YOU RUN WITH?

On another level, do you trust the people who are advocating forced vaccinations? Do you believe they are truthful? Do you trust Bill Gates? Do you trust Anthony Fauci? Do you trust Joe Biden? Do you trust the people who are running our public schools—the ones who are teaching children to ask, "What gender am I?" Do you trust the new transgender "Rachel" Levine whom Joe Biden appointed as our nation's assistant health secretary? We must all choose whom we are going to run with. We are very vulnerable to those we listen to, to those whom we believe. Let us be certain they are trustworthy before we place our confidence in them.

Are these voices telling the truth? This is very important, because we are either believing the truth or a lie.

We are either endorsing the truth or a lie by our behavior.

Further, are we upholding truth? Or are we—by countenancing the contradictory information being broadcast by governmental agencies—bearing false witness?

We were told in the spring of 2020 that two weeks would flatten the curve. Then all society was locked down.

We were told to wear a mask. Then two masks were necessary.

We were told that when the vaccine came, we would no longer need a lockdown or masks. Then when the vaccine arrived and vaccinated people were getting sick, we were told that they wouldn't get as sick as the unvaccinated.

Then we were told that masks were still necessary even if we get the injection.

We were told that the death rates would skyrocket, but they never did.

Illustration: I was recently in a meeting speaking about jurisdictions, and during the Q&A time a man stood up to object to what I was saying and declared that, "People with Covid-19 are lethal weapons." Then a man across the room stood up. This second man was in the funeral home industry. He said that at the beginning of the Covid-19 scare, funeral homes were warned that deaths would skyrocket. The industry was told to be prepared for a massive increase in deaths. But the bodies never materialized. The death rates did not rise.

After a year and a half of observation, I believe that government officials are disseminating false information. Is every person intentionally lying? Probably not. Many are simply repeating the misinformation they were told. But they are still bearing false witness.

The question we face is: Is it loving to bear false witness to our neighbor? Are we loving our neighbor when we promote and support a lie? Are we loving our neighbor by promoting the collectivization of healthcare? Are we loving our neighbor when we endorse known lies? Is it loving to endorse fear?

Governmental institutions and private businesses are misrepresenting the situation with Covid-19, and the story keeps changing. They misrepresent the severity of the cases. They inflate the death rates. They endorse a misleading test. Is it loving to uphold these misrepresentations?

By acquiescing to the misrepresentations and the tyranny, are we exposing other people around us to the lies and the tyranny? Are we affirming the lies? By refusing to expose the lies, we endorse them.

Please don't misunderstand me. I am not suggesting that putting on a mask or getting vaccinated can always be judged as lying. I do think there are occasions where we would wear a mask out of love for our neighbor. If your wife is in the hospital having a baby and the hospital wants you to wear three masks and a hazmat suit, you should suit up. This isn't lying. It's doing what you can to love your wife.

Is wearing a mask bearing false witness? Possibly, possibly not. I wore a mask to get on an airplane. I entered into a written covenant with the airline when I bought my ticket. Before I could finalize the ticket, I had to promise that I would comply with their terms. There are ways that we might wear a mask without bearing false witness. We may be complying under protest.

Yet I am confident of this: loving our neighbor means that we do not endorse lies. Loving our neighbor means that we don't let tyranny continue to advance. It isn't loving to spread unfounded fear and promote governmental overreach.

Alexander Solzhenitsyn was arrested for the last time in 1974. On that day, he released a short essay, "Live Not by Lies." In it he warned the Russian people to renounce the lies they were being told. Here are some excerpts, "the most accessible key to our liberation: a personal nonparticipation in lies! . . .

For when people renounce lies, lies simply cease to exist. Like parasites, they can only survive when attached to a person. . . . Our way must be: Never knowingly support lies! . . . Yes, at first it will not be fair. Someone will have to temporarily lose his job. For the young who seek to live by truth, this will at first severely complicate life, for their tests and quizzes, too, are stuffed with lies, and so choices will have to be made. . . . Not an easy choice for the body, but the only one for the soul. . . . Let us then cower and hunker down, while our comrades the biologists bring closer the day when our thoughts can be read and our genes altered."

We have a biblical and a civic duty before God to protect the family, the church, and the individual from lies. We must protect them even from civil governments when they lie. This is an application of the Ninth Commandment.

We face a powerful foe. We are facing powerful lies. We are watching the world embrace "strong delusions" (2 Thess. 2:11). Let us stand courageously and battle with the weapons the Lord has given us. Let us "live not by lies." Instead, let us live as Paul tells us:

> *"Finally, my brethren, be strong in the Lord and in the power of His might. Put on the whole armor of God"* (Eph. 6:10-11).

—5—

RESISTANCE

Whether you endorse the vaccine or not, the main issue is God's jurisdictional design for your body. Even if you are pro-vaccine, you ought to be against forced vaccinations.

We have a potentially short window of time to declare to our employers and governments that what they are doing is immoral. It's time to speak up loudly and clearly. It's time to educate our employers and governments on matters of the Christian view of the body. And who owns it. It's time to draw a line in the sand and declare who has the authority over what is injected into our bodies. It's time to assert that it is wrong to violate the conscience of a human being on matters that the Bible addresses.

It is time to come out strong in our resistance of tyranny.

Governments and corporate entities have now resorted to bribery and extortion to motivate people to get vaccinated. They are threatening to fire unvaccinated employees. If such people don't resign, employers are threatening to punish them by making them do things no one else is required to do. Recently, Delta Airlines announced they will be charging unvaccinated employees $200.00 per month.[1] United Airlines informed their employees that anyone who requested a medical or religious exemption would be put on unpaid leave.[2] I have heard of doctors in California whose licenses have not been renewed because they approved vaccine exemptions. In North Carolina, the state created a one-million-dollar lottery for those who agreed to be injected.[3] Then they offered $100.00 and a day off work for those who choose to get the shot. Others are offering gift cards. The Krispy Kreme doughnut shop near my house is offering two free doughnuts to vaccinated individuals.

In many ways, the vaccine is a secondary issue. The primary issue is: who has jurisdictional authority over your body? The issue is the collectivization of healthcare. The issue is freedom and glorifying God in our bodies.

A CHRISTIAN'S RESPONSE TO TYRANNY IN THE CORPORATE WORLD

How should we respond to medical tyranny in the workplace? I'd like to make a few recommendations. What follows are

---

1 Karina Mazhukhina, "Delta Air Lines to charge unvaccinated workers $200 monthly. Is it spurring COVID shots?" *Miami Herald*, September 10, 2021, https://www.miamiherald.com/news/nation-world/national/article254139098.html.

2 David Koenig, "United says unvaccinated employees face unpaid leave, termination," *Chicago Sun Times*, September 9, 2021, https://chicago.suntimes.com/business/2021/9/9/22664385/united-airlines-employee-rules-vaccine-requirement-coronavirus-covid-19-travel.

3 Meilin Tompkins, "Are you eligible to win $1 million in the NC COVID-19 vaccine lottery?" WCNC, June 18, 2021, https://www.msn.com/en-us/news/us/are-you-eligible-to-win-241-million-in-the-nc-covid-19-vaccine-lottery/ar-AALbTTd.

some practical considerations regarding what you can do if your employer issues a vaccine mandate.

CONFIRM THE DETAILS OF THE POLICY

First, make sure you understand the details of your company's policy. Some companies are making announcements but have not issued formal policies. Second, look into the details of possible exemptions. There are religious, medical, philosophical, conscientious, moral, legal and ethical exemptions.

DECLARE YOUR POSITION TO YOUR EMPLOYER

Exercise your right of appeal right away. You may be pro-vaccine. Set that aside. There is a greater issue at stake here.

You only have a short window of time for this. I believe that this matter of liberty is so critical at the moment that I'm urging every person who engages me on this subject to make a strong appeal. Declare to your employer that this is morally wrong and that the whole idea of collectivization of healthcare is medically dangerous to millions of people.

In the Bible, Daniel is a wonderful example of this. As mentioned earlier, he refused to follow the king's commands regarding food, but he didn't stop there. He made up his mind to refuse, and then he appealed to the governmental authorities (Dan. 1:8).

The apostle Paul is another example. He appealed to the Word of God, but he also appealed to his right as a Roman citizen (Acts 25:10-11).

By these examples, you can conclude that you can both be a good Christian and a good American citizen at the same time. You can exercise your God-ordained rights and the rights that the Constitution and Bill of Rights and the Civil Rights Act have preserved for you.

COMPLIANCE?

Do not simply roll over and comply. I believe that to quietly comply is the most dangerous position we can take at this time. Compliance allows the cancer of tyranny to grow. The only way to stop tyranny is to resist it.

SPEAK AND WRITE

Here is the most urgent matter: speak and write to your employer about the vaccine mandate (do both). Be respectful. State your case calmly, clearly, and knowledgably. Give information. Use logic. Explain in a dispassionate and gracious way why you are not able to take the vaccine and why it is morally wrong for an employer to demand it.

You should make it clear that what your company is suggesting is contrary to personalized healthcare and incompatible with your duty to protect yourself and your family. Make it plain that your jurisdictional responsibility gives you the freedom of conscience to refuse the vaccine. Let them know that you will not be bribed, you will not be extorted to surrender your authority over your personal medical care.

LIABILITY

Consider engaging your employer in a discussion on the matter of liability. Inquire whether your company is willing to cover your costs in the event of complications from the vaccine. Make it clear that the drug companies are immune from liability. Is your employer willing to accept liability? Where will you go if you become incapacitated for a time or require ongoing medical care due to complications arising from the vaccine?

Should you resign if your employer issues a vaccine mandate?

I would say no. Be patient. Don't jump the gun. Press the proposition. Don't resign. Let your employer grapple with the problem of losing you and others in your company.

I encourage you to continue to appeal to your employer and other employees. Let your employer feel the pressure. Don't quit. Wait for your employer to fire you.

This offers you two points of leverage. First, it sets your employer on his heels to consider the health of his company. Second, it gives you a platform to speak to the present situation. If you are fired, make sure your employment record states your reasons for the conflict and your argument for medical freedom.

TRUST GOD TO WORK HIS WAY IN THIS DIFFICULT SITUATION

What will happen if you refuse a vaccine mandate by your employer? You may lose your job. But you may not. Your employer knows that jobs are very tight. Talent is hard to find. Across the nation and in all occupations, people are quitting. It's difficult and very expensive to replace a good, honest, hard-working employee. Does this describe you? If so, it's quite possible that your employers will be hesitant to terminate you. They may grant you an exemption to the mandate.

I know of companies and hospitals who made announcements for vaccine deadlines but subsequently pushed back the dates. It is possible that these companies were virtue signaling when they issued their mandates. But now they are re-thinking how to deal with the objectors. They may be realizing that they have many valuable employees they don't want to lose. This is why I am encouraging people to resist like a stone wall and wait to see what such resistance accomplishes. Don't give up too soon. Resist hard before you give up.

In summary, I am suggesting that God in His Word has given you jurisdiction over your own body. No one has the right to inject you with chemical substances against your will. You must make the decision for yourself, for the glory of God, and the safety of your family. I might not do what you would do, and vice versa. God has granted each of us this freedom. You now have a window of time to declare the exercise of that freedom. I fear that if we do not do it now, we will have little opportunity later on. It will likely be that we will soon find ourselves on much more dangerous ground.

HOW TO TREAT ONE ANOTHER

It would grieve me if churches and families divided over who gets vaccinated and who does not. Please do not let your hearts move in that direction. This is a matter of personal conscience, conviction and personal jurisdiction. We ought to truly believe this. Each person should engage in "careful studies" and decide for themselves. And please do not bind the consciences of your brethren (Rom. 14:3-5). We are a free people, and we ought to enjoy that freedom. Let there be no first or second class citizens over this matter.

— 6 —

THE TRUTH ABOUT YOU
AND THE AUTHORITY OF GOD

What is the truth about you before the authority of God your Creator? If you are convinced of your jurisdictional authority to receive or reject an injection, there is a more important question that must be addressed. Who is your authority? Do you really believe your body is the temple of the Holy Spirit? Or is this vaccination controversy simply a convenient excuse to disobey authorities? Do you possess the marks of conversion? Is the life of God at work in your soul? Are you convinced that God has a comprehensive claim on your life? Is your whole being under the authority of God, as evidenced by your love for God and obedience to Him? Jesus said, "If you love Me, you will keep My commandments" (see John 14:15).

Are you indifferent to God's ownership of your soul? Isaiah confronted this: "The ox knows its owner and the donkey its master's crib; but Israel does not know, My people do not consider" (Isa. 1:3), as did Paul: "you are not your own" (1 Cor. 6:19-20). Do you know that your life is not your own?

This is a matter of salvation.

Are you unconcerned about the state of your soul? The Bible says, "the soul who sins shall die" (Eze. 18:20). A day is coming when your soul will be required of you. Perhaps even tonight.

How are you caring for your soul? Are you overly concerned about your body and indifferent toward your soul? If you are not concerned about your soul, you ought to ask if you are truly a Christian or if you are simply a conservative who cares about Judeo-Christian values. Are you a sheep or a goat? Are you dead, or have you been born again? Are you "dead to sin and alive to God" (Rom. 6:11)?

Conservatives can get all riled up about all kinds of issues. Conservatives fight for Judeo-Christian values. Yet they may remain unconcerned about their souls.

Are you unconcerned about holiness? The Bible says that without holiness "no one will see the Lord" (Heb. 12:14), and "If you live according to the flesh you will die" (Rom. 8:13).

Are you unchanged by the message of the Gospel? The Bible says, "bear fruits worthy of repentance" (Matt. 3:8).

Are you indifferent to the church? The Bible tells us not to forsake the gathering of ourselves together, "as is the manner of some" (Heb. 10:25). Is the local church at the periphery of your life? Are you intimately involved with a local church? How can you say you love God if you don't love His church?

Are you unconcerned about the means of grace? Are you only casually involved in the preaching of the apostles' doctrine, breaking of bread, prayer, singing, fellowship, and evangelism (Acts 2:42)?

Are you unfocused on the care and feeding of the souls of your wife and children? In Deuteronomy 6 Moses declares that if you love God, and if that love is in your heart, you will teach your children diligently "when you sit in your house, when you walk by the way, when you lie down and when you rise up" (Deut. 6:4-7).

Are you unconcerned about worldly mindedness? The Lord tells us, "Do not love the world or the things in the world" (1 John 2:15) and reminds us that we must be "casting down arguments and every high thing that exalts itself against the knowledge of God, bringing every thought into captivity to the obedience of Christ" (2 Cor. 10:5).

Are you unmoved by the Word of God? Have you ceased to "desire the pure milk of the Word" (1 Pet. 2:2)? Is your soul saying, "it is good for me to draw near to God" (Ps. 73:23-28)?

Do you believe that your body belongs to God, or are you just an anti-vaxxer? When you read the words "you are Mine," does that thrill your soul? Do you embrace God's claim on your whole life, and does it thrill your soul when you read, "you shall have no other gods before Me" (Ex. 20:3)?

If you're going to be an anti-vaxxer; if you renounce government control over your body; if you reject the corporation's right to demand a vaccine, then do you embrace the supreme divine authority? As you consider the issues surrounding forced vaccine mandates, be sure to examine whether you have embraced the authority of God over every part of your life, not just your personal jurisdiction over vaccines. Do you love His laws? Do you want to follow Him? Do you want to uphold His order? Or are you trying to make yourself the supreme authority over your body and life?

When the Bible says, "believe in the Lord Jesus Christ and you will be saved," it means that your whole life belongs to Him. Have you given yourself up to God?

But now, thus says the LORD, who created you, O Jacob, and He who formed you, O Israel: "Fear not, for I have redeemed you; I have called you by your name; You are Mine . . . For I am the LORD your God, the Holy One of Israel, your Savior" (Isaiah 43:1, 3).

Do you love the Lord with your whole heart? Matthew 22:36-40 says:

"Teacher, which is the great commandment in the law?" Jesus said to him, " 'You shall love the LORD your God with all your heart, with all your soul, and with all your mind.' This is the first and great commandment. And the second is like it: 'You shall love your neighbor as yourself.' On these two commandments hang all the Law and the Prophets."

Do you embrace God's claim on your whole life as required in the First Commandment? Exodus 20:3, "You shall have no other gods before Me."

This includes everything. Everything you think with your mind. Everything you do with your hands.

Everything you say with your mouth. Everything you feel in your heart. Everything you intend with your will. Everything you see with your eyes. Everywhere you go with your feet.

Everything you ingest and inject into your body.

You have been created by God. You have been made in His image. You belong to Him. This is God's claim on your life.

While considering the authorities demanding vaccinations, remember that our Lord Jesus Christ is the King of kings and Lord of lords.